Carmen Suite

Classical Guitar Arrangements from Bizet's Opera "Carmen"

Néstor Ausqui

Special Thanks to:
Sam Butler, Avid Technologies, United Kingdom
Mr. John Grado, Grado Labs, Brooklyn, New York
John D'Addario, Jr., D'Addario Corporation

WWW.MELBAY.COM

Preface

One might think that it would be impossible to arrange the music of Georges Bizet's opera, *Carmen* —for solo classic guitar. The obvious challenge is: Will the guitar be able to emulate the tone color or character of music originally composed for orchestral instrumentation?

Although the guitar is an intimate, sweet and pleasant-sounding instrument, it also has a great timbral potential that instantly identifies and distinguishes itself from other instruments. Without a doubt, these characteristics make the guitar the ideal instrument to reflect both the character and sensuality of the dances that occur throughout Bizet's opera.

By coming to that conclusion in the 21st century, there is the risk of perhaps forgetting the value the guitar had in the music of the 19th century. It is well known that after Beethoven, it was Hector Berlioz who gave the orchestra a new luster through his genius as an orchestrator. Although Berlioz himself was a guitarist, there is no documentation of his having said, *'The guitar is a small orchestra."* This controversial phrase, regardless of who may have said it, clearly expresses how significant and amazing this instrument can be.

Actually, it was a Berlioz contemporary, Dionisio Aguado, who first referred to the guitar as a "miniature orchestra." The phrase occurs in Aguado's *New Method for Guitar* of 1843; in Part One —Theory & Practice, Chapter I, "The concept that one should form about the guitar," Aguado writes:

> The guitar is an instrument that is not yet well known. Who would say that of all those instruments in use today, it is perhaps the most likely to give the illusion of similarity to the effects of *a miniature orchestra*? This seems inconceivable at first glance; nonetheless, experience leaves no doubt about it.*

So then, without a doubt, in Néstor Ausqui's arrangements of the music from Bizet's *Carmen,* it is the guitar that takes over the sound; it both sings like a human voice and accompanies itself, giving the work an irrefutable *guitar identity.*

The presence of Spanish, i.e., Gypsy, dance can be considered as a *Leitmotif* present throughout *Carmen.* The erotic gestures of the habanera, the strong corporal rhythms of the Danse Boheme, or the aggressive virtuosity of the Aragonaise—all dances that were exotic for the Paris of 1875—transcend from the body to the music in a paradigmatic way. The peculiar feeling manifested in Spanish dance is now expressed through the guitar with a full and defined instrumental identity.

Guillermo René Alvarez
Musicologist, Professor at the Instituto Superior de Música.
Universidad Nacional del Litoral-Argentina

---

*Dionisio Aguado, 'Nuevo Método para Guitarra', Año 1843, **Parte Primera Teórico –Práctica, Capítulo I, Idea que se debe formar de la guitarra,** *1- La guitarra es instrumento que aún no está bien conocido. ¿Quién diría que de todos los que se usan hoy, tal vez, es el más a propósito para causar ilusión con la semejanza de los efectos de una orquesta en miniatura? Inconcebible parece esto a primera vista; sin embargo, la experiencia no deja duda de ello.*

Contents

Argonaise

Georges Bizet
arreglo Néstor Ausqui

Marcato ed energico
Pizz.
pizz.
pizz.
rit.
seco
sfz
cresc.
seco

Habanera

⑥ = D
Georges Bizet
arreglo Néstor Ausqui
Allegretto quasi andantino ♩ = 72
solista

14
Harm.
19

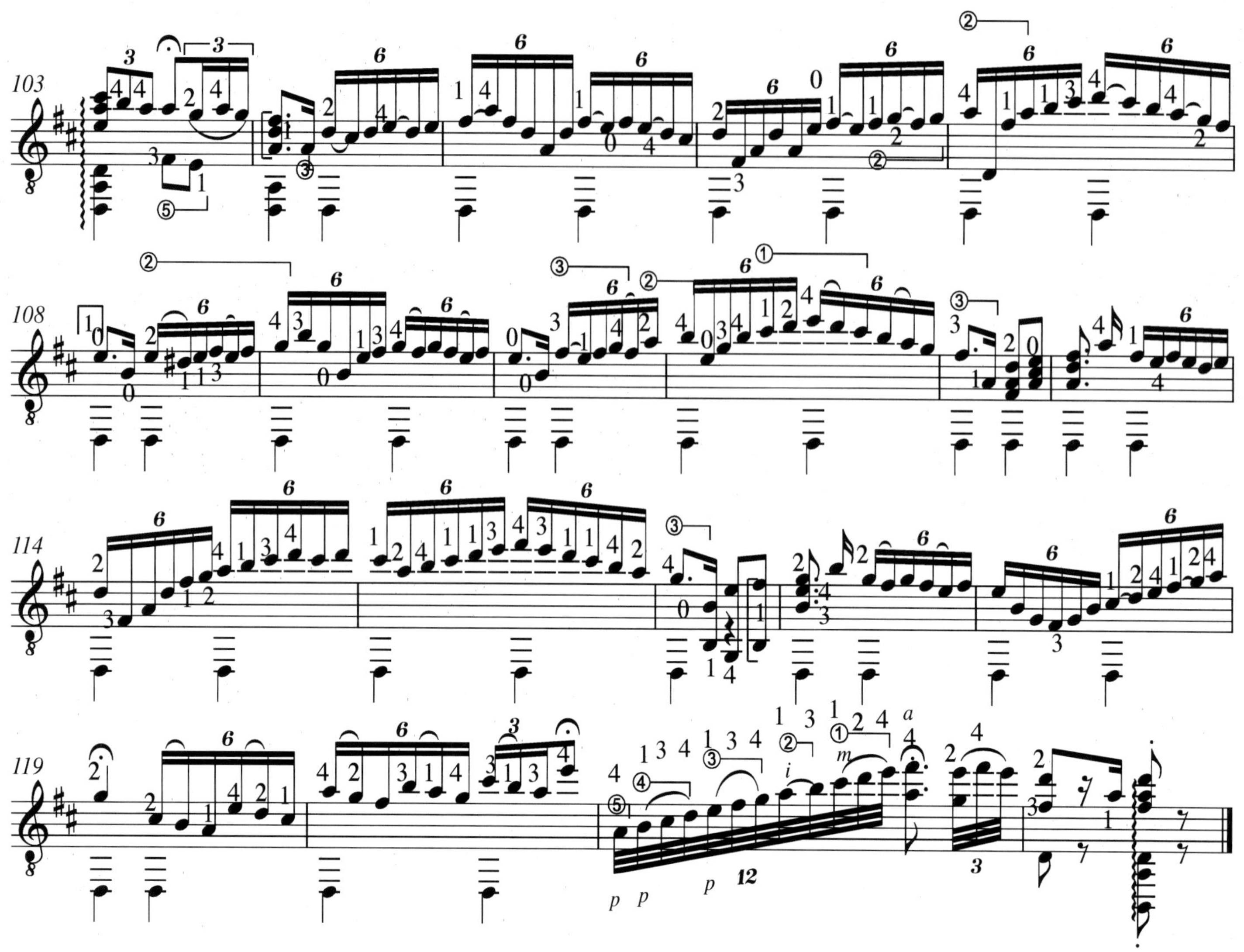

This page has been left blank to avoid an awkward page turn.

Seguidillas

Georges Bizet
arreglo Néstor Ausqui

VIII
Cadenza
III
II
VII
a m i

143
3
2
1
2
4
2
②
3
4
3
⑥
3
3
3

Chant de la Mort

Georges Bizet
arreglo Néstor Ausqui

This page has been left blank to avoid an awkward page turn.

Danse Bohéme

Georges Bizet
arreglo Néstor Ausqui

m i m a
rit.

tuta forza
Secco

Other Mel Bay Classical Guitar Solo Collections